SOCIAL SKILLS FOR TEEN GIRLS 13-19

A Survival Guide With 30+ Activities to Boost
your Morale, Make Friends, Improve Social Life,
Self Confidence and Self Esteem

by

Teresa C.
Prime Pen Publisher

Disclaimer Notice

This book is written and published independently. Please keep in mind that the material in this publication is solely for educational and entertaining purposes. All efforts have provided authentic, up-to-date, trustworthy, and comprehensive information. There are no express or implied assurances. The purpose of this book's material is to assist readers in having a better understanding of the subject matter. The activities, information, and exercises are provided solely for self-help information. This book is not intended to replace expert psychologists, legal, financial, or other guidance. If you require counseling, please get in touch with a qualified professional.

By reading this text, the reader accepts that the author will not be held liable for any damages, indirectly or directly, experienced due to the use of the information included herein, particularly, but not limited to, omissions, errors, or inaccuracies. As a reader, you are accountable for your decisions, actions, and consequences.

AUTHOR BIO

Teresa C. is a clinical psychologist and an author who is committed to assisting young people in developing core social skills that will help them become independent adults and enrich their lives. She made it her mission to support teenagers as they navigate the vital era of adolescence and aid in their successful transition into adulthood.

CONTENTS

MY SUCCESS STORY

My name is Teresa, and I'm here to share with you my success story about my journey with improved social skills. When I was a teenager, I struggled to connect with my peers and assert myself in social situations. I often felt shy and unsure of myself, leading to missed opportunities and strained relationships with others.

One day, I had the chance to attend a youth leadership conference where I met a group of dynamic and confident young women. I was amazed by their ability to communicate effectively, build rapport with others, and assert themselves respectfully and confidently. Inspired by their example, I made a commitment to improve my own social skills and build stronger relationships with others.

Through my involvement in extracurricular activities, volunteering, and seeking out positive role models and mentors, I gradually developed my social skills and gained the confidence and self-assurance to pursue my goals. I learned how to communicate effectively, listen actively, build empathy and understanding, and assert myself respectfully in social situations. These skills not only helped me build stronger relationships with others but also enabled me to excel academically and pursue my passions with greater confidence and focus.

I am happy to share that I now enjoy a vibrant social life where I can confidently share my thoughts and feelings with others without feeling embarrassed.

To all the teen girls out there struggling with their social skills, I want to encourage you to take a chance, seek out mentors and push against the obstacles that stand in your way. You, too, can enjoy the sweet rewards that come with improved social skills. "Social Skills for Teen Girls" is a comprehensive guide that is specifically written for teen girls.This book provides practical advice and strategies and 30+ for developing and strengthening social skills in teenage girls.

INTRODUCTION : UNLEASHING YOUR SOCIAL POTENTIAL AS A TEEN GIRL

Have you ever felt nervous in social situations with your peers?

Do you want to discover how to build confidence and improve social skills?

As a teenage girl, social skills are a vital aspect of your personal growth and development. Whether you're trying to make new friends, build meaningful relationships, or simply communicate more effectively with those around you, strong social skills can help you navigate the complex social world of adolescence with greater ease and confidence. Whether you're struggling to fit in at school, feeling shy in social situations, or simply looking for ways to improve your social skills, this guide is the perfect resource to help you take control of your social life and build the skills you need to succeed.

Developing strong social skills takes time and effort, but the rewards are significant. By improving your ability to connect with others and communicating effectively, you can build stronger relationships, experience greater self-confidence, and achieve greater success in both your personal and professional life. In this book, you will explore 30+ activities to help you develop the social skills you need to thrive as a teenage girl. From building confidence and self-esteem to making new friends and improving your communication skills, these activities will help you build the social skills you need to succeed in every area of your life. Social skills are also critical for good mental and emotional well-being. According to research, those with good social skills are more likely to feel good emotions, are less likely to experience despair and anxiety and are generally happier.

Conversely, a lack of social skills can lead to social isolation, conflict, and negative mental health outcomes. For example, if you struggle to communicate effectively or resolve conflicts with others, you may find yourself feeling lonely, anxious, or depressed. This can significantly impact your mental and emotional well-being and make it harder for you to succeed in other areas of life. As a teenager, I watched a close friend of mine go through a transformational journey in her social skills development. My friend, Rachel, had always struggled with anxiety and shyness in social situations. She would often struggle to initiate conversations or speak up for herself, and as a result, found it difficult to make new friends or assert herself in group settings. However, Rachel was determined to improve her social skills and overcome her anxiety. She began by joining a local youth group, where she met like-minded individuals who shared her passions and interests. Through her involvement in the group, Rachel developed her communication skills and learned how to listen actively to others. She also built her confidence in initiating conversations and speaking up in group discussions. With her mentor's help and her family's support, Rachel continued to develop her social skills, focusing on building empathy and understanding others' perspectives. She learned how to navigate complex social situations with grace and compassion, building meaningful relationships with her peers and creating a sense of belonging in her community. Rachel's story is a testament to the power of developing social skills, even in the face of significant challenges. Through her determination and perseverance, she overcame her anxiety and built the foundation for healthy relationships and personal growth. Her story serves as an inspiration for teenagers everywhere to focus on developing their social skills and creating meaningful connections with others.

Ultimately, the goal of this book is to provide you with a comprehensive guide to developing essential social skills, one that can help you thrive both in your personal life and in the broader world. So, whether you're an introverted teen struggling to make new friends or a social butterfly looking to take your social life to the next level, this book has something to offer everyone. In the following chapters, we'll cover a range of topics, including boosting confidence and self-esteem, making new friends, improving communication skills, and improving social life. We'll also provide practical tips and activities designed to help you build your skills and put them into practice in your everyday life.

So, let's get started.

CHAPTER 1 : SOCIAL SKILLS : A SECRET WEAPON FOR SUCCESS

Being a teenager can be an exciting and challenging time, especially when it comes to social situations. Whether you're at school, with friends, or meeting new people, having strong social skills is essential for building positive relationships and feeling confident in social situations. In this chapter, we'll explore the basic concept of social skills, their importance, and some practical ways to improve your social skills as a teen girl. When we think about the traits that lead to success in life, qualities like intelligence, talent, and hard work often come to mind. But there's another important factor that is sometimes overlooked: social skills. Having strong social skills can be a secret weapon for success in many areas of life.

First and foremost, strong social skills can help you build positive relationships with others. Whether working in a team or simply making friends, communicating effectively and building rapport with others is essential. This can help you achieve your goals or simply feel more connected to the people around you.

Strong social skills can also help you navigate difficult situations with grace. Whether you're dealing with conflict or simply trying to communicate effectively with someone who sees things differently, being able to listen actively, express yourself clearly, and read the body language and emotions of others can make all the difference.

Strong social skills can help you build self-confidence and resilience. By mastering the art of communication, you'll feel more comfortable and capable in social situations and be better equipped to handle challenges when they arise.

1.1 Understanding Social Skills

Social skills refer to a set of abilities and behaviors that allow individuals to interact effectively with others in social situations. These skills include a range of communication abilities, such as verbal and nonverbal communication, active listening, showing empathy, and assertiveness. Developing and strengthening social skills is an ongoing process that can involve a range of strategies and activities, from practicing active listening to participating in group activities and building a supportive network of friends. With time and practice, individuals can develop strong social skills that serve them well in all areas of life. Effective communication is one of the essential aspects of social skills. Good communication means being able to express yourself effectively, but it also means being able to listen to others and understand their perspectives. In order to communicate well, it's important to be clear, concise, and respectful in your interactions with others. Social skills are important for a range of personal situations, including making friends, networking, and building relationships. Good social skills can lead to a more fulfilling life, as individuals who possess these skills are often seen as more trustworthy, likable, and effective in their roles. Social skills can be developed and improved through practice and feedback. Individuals can learn social skills by observing others, receiving guidance and feedback from mentors, participating in social activities, and taking part in skill-building workshops or classes.

1.2 Why Social Skills are Crucial: A Deep Dive

Social skills are essential for building healthy relationships and communicating effectively with others. As a teenage girl, strong social skills are particularly important. They can help you make friends, work well in groups, resolve conflicts, and develop positive relationships with teachers, mentors, and peers. Social skills are also critical for success in many aspects of life, including education, career, and personal growth. Strong social skills can boost your self-confidence, improve your ability to handle stress, and increase your overall well-being. Furthermore, research has shown that those with strong social skills are happier, more successful, and have better overall mental and physical health. Social skills are crucial for a variety of reasons. Here are a few reasons why social skills are important for you:

• Building and Maintaining Friendships:

Making and keeping friends is one of the most crucial components of life. Good social skills can help you build and maintain healthy relationships with your peers. This can help you feel more connected, supported, and happy.

• Developing Communication Skills:

Social skills also help you develop communication skills, which are essential for success in both personal and professional relationships. Effective communication skills can help you express your thoughts and ideas clearly, listen actively to others, and work collaboratively with others.

• Developing Self-Confidence:

Social skills can help you develop self-confidence by allowing you to feel more comfortable in social situations. With good social skills, you can approach new people and situations with ease and feel more comfortable expressing yourself.

• Developing Emotional Intelligence:

Social skills also help you develop emotional intelligence, which is the ability to recognize, understand, and manage your own emotions, as well as the emotions of others. This can help you develop stronger and more meaningful relationships with others and navigate difficult social situations more easily.

- **Enhancing Leadership Skills:**

Good social skills can also enhance your leadership skills. With strong social skills, you can inspire and motivate others, build strong teams, and work effectively with others to achieve common goals.

- **Strengthening Resilience:**

Developing good social skills can help you become more resilient to life's challenges, setbacks, and failures. You'll have a supportive network of family, friends, and peers who can help you through difficult times. By practicing good social skills, you'll learn how to cope with stress and manage your emotions effectively, making you more resilient in the face of adversity.

- **Promoting Diversity and Inclusion:**

Social skills can help you appreciate diversity and understand different perspectives. You'll learn to respect and accept others, regardless of their background, culture, or beliefs, which can foster a more inclusive and tolerant society. You'll be able to communicate effectively with people from all walks of life, and your ability to connect with others will be enhanced.

- **Improving Mental Health:**

Developing strong social skills can support your mental health by giving you a sense of belonging, support, and connection. You'll be less likely to experience mental health problems like depression and anxiety. By building strong relationships with others, you'll feel more confident and secure in yourself and better equipped to handle the challenges of adolescence.

- **Supporting Academic Success:**

Good social skills can support your academic success by improving communication with teachers, peers, and classmates. You'll be able to express yourself clearly, listen actively, and collaborate effectively, which can help you achieve your academic goals. By developing strong social skills, you'll also be more likely to form study groups and participate in extracurricular activities, which can help you succeed in school.

1.3 From Shy to Confident: How Social Skills can assist You Break Out of your Shell

As a teen girl, you may feel like you're stuck in a shell, afraid to come out and show the world who you really are. But developing social skills can help you break out of that shell and shine like the unique and amazing person you are. Here are some examples of how social skills can help you break out of your shell:

- **Speak Up and Be Heard:**

Have you ever been in a group discussion and felt too shy or intimidated to share your thoughts? By developing social skills such as assertiveness and effective communication, you can learn to speak up and be heard. Imagine if you were in a class debate and could express your opinion confidently and persuasively. Not only would you feel proud of yourself, but your classmates would see you in a new light and recognize your intelligence and insight.

- **Connect with Others:**

Making connections with others can be challenging, especially if you're shy or introverted. But by developing social skills such as active listening and empathy, you can learn to connect with others on a deeper level. Imagine if you were at a social event and could have a meaningful conversation with someone you just met. Not only would you feel more comfortable and confident, but you may even make a new friend or mentor.

- **Overcome Fears and Obstacles:**

Breaking out of your shell often means confronting fears and obstacles that may hold you back. By developing social skills such as problem-solving and resilience, you can learn to overcome these challenges and emerge more robust and more confident. Imagine being asked to present in front of your class, but you were afraid of public speaking. By using your social skills to prepare and practice, you could overcome your fear and deliver a successful presentation that impresses your classmates and teachers.

- **Explore New Opportunities:**

Breaking out of your shell means experiencing new things and stepping outside of your comfort bubble trying new things .By developing social skills such as open-mindedness and curiosity, you can learn to embrace new opportunities and experiences. Imagine if you were invited to a club meeting for a group that you're interested in, but you're nervous about attending. Using your social skills to introduce yourself and engage with others, you could discover a new passion and make new friends.

1.4 Mind-Blowing Ways to Improve Your Social Skills

Remember, the key to improving your social skills is to practice and try new things. Don't be afraid to make mistakes or experience some discomfort, as this is a natural part of the learning process. By taking the initiative to improve your social skills, you can build your confidence, expand your social network, and enhance your overall quality of life. Making friends, getting out, and meeting new people are not always simple for everyone. Some people tend to steer clear of social settings because they can feel anxious or uncomfortable. Some people prefer their alone time to just being surrounded by others because they are naturally introverted. Whichever group you fit into, it's still preferable to have strong interpersonal skills and efficient communication techniques. The ability to interact and connect with others depends on having strong social skills. The development of friendships and a more satisfying path through life both depend on this. It might be astonishing how many chances come your way and how many doors open up in life when you have strong social skills. How can you now grow and enhance those skills?

Following are some ways to improve your social skills

- **Volunteer:**

Volunteering can provide a variety of opportunities to improve your social skills, such as working in a team, communicating with others, and developing leadership skills. You can volunteer at local organizations, such as hospitals, nursing homes, or community centers, or you can volunteer for causes that you're passionate about. Volunteering can also help you gain new experiences and perspectives, which can make you a more well-rounded and interesting person to talk to.

- **Join a Club or Group:**

Joining a club or group can help you find new friends who share your interests and values.

You can join a club or group that aligns with your hobbies, such as a sports team, music club, or drama club, or you can join a group that focuses on a specific cause, such as a volunteer group or activist organization. Participating in group activities can help you develop your communication, teamwork, and leadership skills and give you a sense of belonging and purpose.

- **Attend Social Events:**

Attending social events, such as parties or community events, can help you practice your social skills in a relaxed and fun setting. You can work on your small talk skills by introducing yourself to new people and engaging in conversation, or you can work on your social confidence by stepping out of your comfort zone and trying new things.

- **Work on Your Body Language:**

Your body language can impact how others perceive you. For example, standing tall with good posture can make you appear confident and approachable. Practicing good eye contact and smiling can also help you to connect with others.

- **Practice Mindfulness:**

The practice of mindfulness entails being fully present in the moment without distraction or judgment. You may improve your awareness of your own feelings and thoughts by engaging in mindfulness practices, which will make it easier for you to understand the needs of others. You can practice mindfulness by taking deep breaths, meditating, or doing yoga. This can help you stay calm and focused in social situations and make others feel more comfortable around you.

1.5 How Social Skills Impact Your Personal and Academic Life?

Social skills are a key aspect of your personal and academic life as a teen girl. By developing strong social skills, you can build deeper connections with others, communicate more effectively, and navigate the challenges of adolescence with greater ease. In turn, these skills can also help you perform better academically and build a strong support network that will be beneficial throughout your life.

- **Personal Life:**

✓ Developing strong social skills as a teen girl can have a profound impact on many aspects of your life. In your personal life, strong social skills can help you navigate the complexities of relationships and social interactions. You'll be better able to form new friendships, deepen existing ones, and communicate more effectively with family members, classmates, and others in your life.

✓ Good social skills can also help you build self-confidence, reduce social anxiety, and develop a positive self-image. As you become more skilled at interacting with others, you'll feel more comfortable in social situations, which might enhance the general state of your mental health and well-being. This can be especially important during the teenage years, which can be a time of significant social and emotional changes.

✓ Building good social skills can help you better understand others and see things from different perspectives. This can improve your empathy and make you a more compassionate and understanding person. It can also help you avoid conflicts and misunderstandings with others.

✓ Social skills can also help you develop resilience and coping strategies for dealing with the ups and downs of life. When you're able to communicate your feelings and ask for help when you need it, you're less likely to feel overwhelmed or alone in difficult situations.

- **Academic life:**

✓ Strong social skills can help you form study groups or find study partners, which can improve your learning outcomes. By working with others who have different strengths and weaknesses, you can learn from one another and fill in gaps in your own understanding.

✓ Developing good social skills can help you participate more effectively in class discussions and group projects. By being able to express your ideas clearly and listen to others, you may participate in the learning process and improve your grasp of the subject matter.

✓ Good social skills can also help you build a network of academic support, including teachers, counselors, and academic advisors. By being able to communicate your needs and seek help when necessary, you can improve your academic performance.

1.6 Top Social Skills You Need to Succeed in Life.

You may position yourself for success in every aspect of your life by developing good social skills. Whether you're pursuing academic achievements or building meaningful relationships, these skills can help you navigate social situations with greater ease and build greater confidence and resilience.

Following are some top social skills you need to succeed in life

- **Active Listening:**

Listening actively and attentively to others is an essential social skill that can help you build strong relationships. For example, if your friend is upset about a problem they're facing, you can listen to them actively by maintaining eye contact, asking open-ended questions, and showing empathy.

- **Communication :**

Effective communication is critical in all aspects of life, and it's essential for teenagers. You can practice communication skills by speaking clearly and concisely, maintaining eye contact, and using appropriate body language.

- **Empathy:**

Being able to understand and share the feelings of others is a valuable social skill that can help you build strong relationships. For example, if your friend is struggling, you can show empathy by acknowledging their feelings and offering support.

- **Conflict Resolution:**

Conflict is a part of life, but resolving conflicts positively and constructively is a valuable social skill. You may work on your conflict resolution skills by attentively listening to the other person's point of view, expressing your own views in a cool, courteous manner, and collaborating to come up with a solution that benefits all sides.

- **Respect:**

Treating others respectfully is an essential social skill that can help you build positive relationships. You can demonstrate respect by being polite, using good manners, and considering others' feelings.

- **Open-Mindedness:**

Being open-minded means being willing to consider different perspectives and ideas. This social skill can help you build strong relationships and expand your worldview. You can practice open-mindedness by being receptive to new ideas, listening to other's perspectives, and being willing to learn from others.

- **Collaboration:**

In many areas of life, from school projects to extracurricular activities, collaboration is essential for achieving success. Collaborating effectively involves sharing ideas, working through challenges, and contributing to a common goal. When you develop strong collaboration skills, you can work effectively with others and achieve greater success than you could alone.

1.7 The Role of Social Skills in Building a Positive Self Image.

Social skills play a critical role in building a positive self-image. Positive self-image refers to the way an individual views themselves, their worth, and their capabilities. When an individual has strong social skills, they are better equipped to navigate social situations and build positive relationships, which can contribute to a positive self-image. Good social skills involve the ability to communicate effectively with others, understand and empathize with their emotions and needs, and build positive relationships. When individuals have these skills, they are more likely to be able to express themselves confidently and assertively, understand and respond to the feelings and needs of others, and build positive connections with the people around them. On the other hand, poor social skills can lead to negative interactions, social isolation, and feelings of rejection, which can erode an individual's self-image and confidence over time. Therefore, social skills are essential for creating a sense of belonging and social support and boosting self-esteem and confidence. They can contribute to an individual's overall sense of well-being and help them to lead a more fulfilling life. Social skills are important not only for building positive relationships with others but also for the relationship we have with ourselves. When we interact positively with others, we tend to feel better about ourselves and our abilities, which can translate into a more positive self-image. Additionally, having strong social skills can help individuals to navigate difficult social situations, such as conflict resolution or dealing with difficult personalities. When we feel confident, and in control in these situations, it can further contribute to a positive self-image.

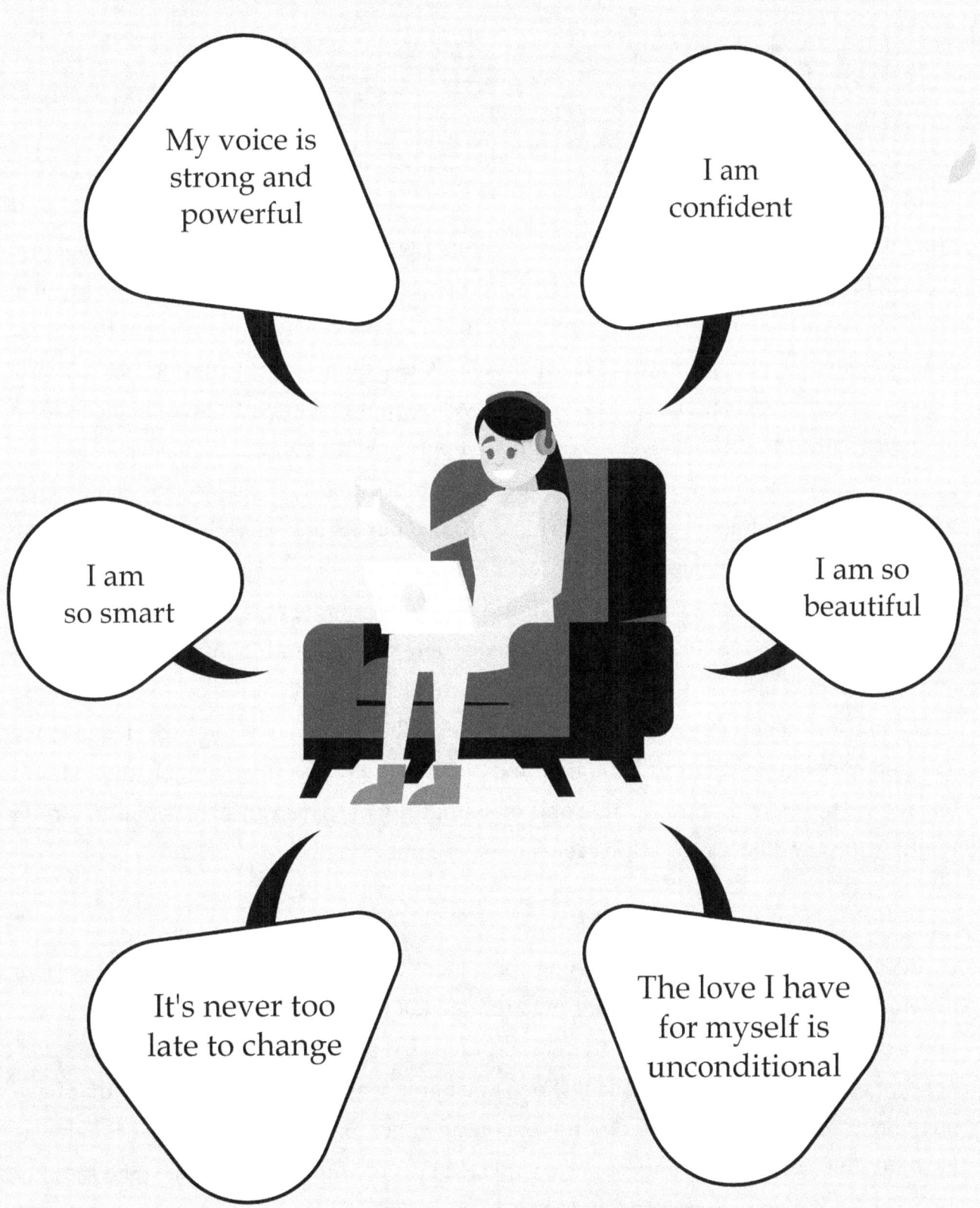

CHAPTER 2: LIFTING YOURSELF UP: BOOSTING YOUR MORALE FOR A BETTER YOU!

High morale is a term used to describe a feeling of well-being, optimism, and confidence. It is characterized by a feeling of direction in life, self-worth, and a positive perspective. A strong sense of self-worth, pride in one's achievements, and optimism about the future are all examples of high morale. High morale is essential since it may improve many facets of our life. When our morale is high, we are more inclined to face obstacles with an upbeat attitude and persevere through adversities. High morale can also enhance our physical and mental well-being. We frequently experience less stress, worry, and despair when we feel good about ourselves. This can raise our feeling of well-being as a whole and result in a more rewarding existence. High morale and social skills are closely linked; as having strong social skills can contribute to higher morale and vice versa. When we have high morale, we tend to approach social interactions with confidence, positivity, and optimism. This can make us more approachable, enjoyable to be around, and more likely to form positive relationships with others. When we have strong social skills, we can better communicate our thoughts and feelings, express ourselves positively, and engage with others in a productive and meaningful way. This can help us build strong relationships and boost our self-esteem and sense of belonging.

Inspiring Story to Boost Your Morale

As a teen girl, it's natural to feel nervous or unsure in social situations but it's important to remember that everyone has their own unique talents and abilities, and it's okay to be yourself. Sarah was a bit of an introvert and often felt shy around new people. One day, her school decided to put on a talent show, and Sarah was convinced that she didn't have any talents to showcase. But her friends encouraged her to give it a try. At first, Sarah was hesitant, but with the support of her friends, she decided to take a chance. She thought about her hobbies and interests and remembered that she loved to write poetry. Sarah had never shared her poetry with anyone, but she decided to perform one of her poems at the talent show. The night of the talent show arrived, and Sarah took to the stage, feeling nervous but excited. As she began to recite her poem, she felt her confidence growing. Her voice grew stronger, and the audience was captivated by her words. When she finished, the crowd erupted into applause. After the talent show, many of her classmates came up to her to tell her how much they enjoyed her poem. Some even asked her to write poems for them. Sarah was overjoyed by the positive feedback and realized that others appreciated her unique talent. From that day on, Sarah's confidence grew, and she began to feel more comfortable in social situations. She learned that it's okay to be yourself and share your talents with others, even if it feels scary at first. With the support of friends, anything is possible. Remember, you are unique and have your own special talents and abilities. Embrace them and share them with the world. You never know whom you might inspire or how much of a positive impact you can make on others.

2.1 What's Eating at You? Identifying the Root Cause of Low Morale

Dear teenage girls,

Growing up as a teenage girl can be challenging, and it's not uncommon to experience low morale or feelings of self-doubt at times. Keep in mind that you are not alone and that it is appropriate to seek assistance when you need it. By recognizing the causes of low morale and taking steps to address them, you can overcome these challenges and thrive as a confident, empowered teenage girl.

Following are some causes of low self-esteem

- **Academic Pressure**

Academic pressure is one of the most common causes of low morale for teenage girls. You may feel like you are not doing enough or that you need to excel in everything you do. Remember that it's okay to make mistakes, and it's not healthy to put too much pressure on yourself. Talk to your teachers or parents about your academic concerns, and seek support if needed.

- **Social Pressure**

Social pressure can also contribute to low morale. You may feel like you need to fit in or conform to specific standards of beauty or behavior. However, it's important to remember that you are unique and that it's okay to be yourself. Surround yourself with friends who accept and support you for who you are, and don't be afraid to set boundaries and say "no" to things that make you feel uncomfortable.

- ## Body Image

Body image is another common cause of low morale for teenage girls. You may feel self-conscious about your appearance or compare yourself to others. However, it's important to understand that beauty comes in many different forms and that how you feel about yourself is ultimately what matters. Focus on taking care of your body by eating healthy and staying active, and remember that your appearance does not determine your worth.

- ## Family Issues

Family issues and mental health concerns can also contribute to low morale. If you are dealing with a difficult family situation or struggling with your mental health, seek professional help and support from a trusted adult or mental health professional.

2.2 Rise Above: Strategies for Boosting Your Morale

The teenage years can come with a lot of challenges, including academic pressures, social dynamics, and changes in your body and mind. Boosting your morale can help you feel more confident and resilient as you navigate these challenges.

Here are some strategies you can try:

- ## Practice Self-Care:

Self-care is all about looking after your body, mind, and spirit while maintaining an active lifestyle. Spend time engaging in enjoyable activities, such as taking a bath, going for a walk, or doing yoga. To help you relax and lower tension, you might also try journaling or meditation.

- ## Build a Support System:

You might feel more self-assured and driven by surrounding yourself with positive and encouraging individuals. Find people who you can trust and who will listen to you without judgment. You can also seek out mentors or role models who inspire you.

- **Set Achievable Goals:**

Setting goals can give you a sense of purpose and help you stay motivated. Make sure to set goals that are specific, measurable, achievable, relevant, and time-bound (SMART). Divide more challenging objectives into smaller, more achievable steps, and acknowledge your accomplishments along the way.

- **Challenge Negative Thoughts:**

Everyone occasionally has negative thoughts, but it's crucial to avoid letting them stop you from moving forward. Challenge negative thoughts by questioning their accuracy and replacing them with positive affirmations. For example, if you're thinking, "I'm not good enough," remind yourself of your past accomplishments or focus on your strengths.

- **Practice Mindfulness**

Mindfulness entails being present at the moment without judgment. You can practice mindfulness by focusing on your breath, paying attention to your surroundings, or using a guided meditation app. Mindfulness can help you reduce stress and anxiety and increase feelings of calmness.

2.3 Lifting Your Spirits: The Ultimate Toolkit for Boosting Your Morale

Following are some activities to boost your morale:

- **Heartfelt Gratitude Journaling**

✓ Keeping a gratitude journal can be an effective way to boost morale and improve your overall well-being. You may create a more positive outlook and enhance your capacity to deal with obstacles by emphasizing the good things in your life and showing gratitude to others. Following are steps to perform this activity

✓ Select a notebook or journal that you enjoy writing in and that you will feel comfortable using regularly.

✓ Create a title page for your gratitude journal that reflects your intention to practice gratitude. You can include your name, the date, and any other design elements that are meaningful to you.

✓ Set a goal for how often you want to write in your journal, such as daily or weekly.

✓ At the start of each writing session, take a few deep breaths to settle your thoughts and bring your attention to the present.

✓ Write down 2-4 things that you are grateful for. These can be big or small and can include people, experiences, or things that you appreciate in your life.

✓ If you are struggling to think of things to be grateful for, try to focus on specific aspects of your day, such as the sun shining, a warm cup of tea, or a kind word from a friend.

✓ Be consistent with your gratitude practice writing in your journal regularly. This can help make gratitude a habit and increase the benefits of the practice over time.

My Daily Heartfelt Gratitude Journal

Date:

Five things that I appreciate in my life:

1: _____

2: _____

3: _____

4: _____

5: _____

Four things that I'm excited about in the near future:

1: _____

2: _____

3: _____

4: _____

Three things that I achieved today:

1: _____

2: _____

3: _____

Two people who I feel grateful to have in my life:

1: _____

2: _____

One incredible event that happened this week that made me feel happy or proud:

_____

_____

_____

_____

_____

_____

- **Positive Affirmation Station.**

Positive affirmations can help boost your morale and improve your overall well-being.

Here are some steps to perform this activity:

✓ Breathe a few times deeply and clear your mind of any negative thoughts or distractions. Sit or stand in a comfortable and quiet space where you feel relaxed and focused.

✓ Think about the qualities you want to cultivate in yourself or the areas of your life you want to improve.

✓ Set a positive intention for your affirmations, such as "I am open to positive change" or "I am ready to manifest my dreams."

✓ Select 3-5 affirmations that resonate with you and that you can believe in. Make them short, specific, and in the present tense, such as "I am confident and capable" or "I choose to focus on the good in my life."

✓ Read your affirmations aloud to yourself with intention and conviction. Repeat each affirmation several times, focusing on the meaning behind the words and allowing yourself to feel their positive energy.

Positive Affirmation Station

Name: _____ Date: _____

Write your affirmations and when you plan to use them below, using the following steps:

- Start your affirmations with "I am..."

- Use present tense and positive language.

- Keep your affirmations brief.

- Make sure your affirmations are specific and personal

My affirmations:

1. I will use this when: _____
2. _____
3. _____
4. _____
5. _____
6. _____
7. _____
8. _____
9. _____
10. _____
11. _____
12. _____
13. _____
14. _____
15. _____

I will use this when:

1. _____
2. _____
3. _____
4. _____
5. _____
6. _____
7. _____
8. _____
9. _____
10. _____
11. _____
12. _____
13. _____
14. _____
15. _____

- ## Goal-Setting Genius

Goal-setting activities can be incredibly important for boosting morale, as they provide a clear path for individuals to follow in order to achieve their desired outcomes. Setting goals gives us a clear sense of direction and purpose. It helps us to focus our efforts on achieving the things that matter most to us, which can increase our motivation and sense of fulfillment.

Here are the steps for a goal-setting activity:

✓ Start by reflecting on your values and what's important to you. This will help you identify goals that align with your beliefs and desires.

✓ Identify a specific and measurable goal that you want to achieve. It's important to be specific and clear about what you want to accomplish

✓ Break down your goal into smaller, more achievable steps. This will make you stay motivated.

✓ Create a plan to achieve your goal. Make a list of the actions you must perform, the materials you require, and the due dates for each action.

✓ Stay accountable by tracking your progress regularly. This can help you stay motivated and make adjustments to your plan as needed.

Goal Setting Genius

MY GOAL	Why is this important to me?

Breaking it Down

STEP 1	STEP 2	STEP 3	STEP 4

What obstacles might I encounter?		Strategies for Overcoming obstacles
	→	
	→	
	→	

How will I keep myself accountable and track progress?

What will I do each day?	When will I achieve my goal?

• My Self-Care Plan

Self-care is crucial for boosting morale because it allows teen girls to prioritize their own physical, emotional, and mental health. Taking the time to care for oneself can help reduce stress and prevent burnout, and it can also help individuals to feel more confident, relaxed and refreshed.Following are the steps for a self-care activity:

✓ Start by carving out dedicated time for self-care on a regular basis, whether it's daily, weekly, or some other schedule that works for you.

✓ Identify activities that you enjoy and that promote your well-being. This could include exercise, mindfulness, creative pursuits, or anything else that helps you feel relaxed and renewed.

✓ Create a self-care plan or schedule that includes the activities you have identified. Make sure to prioritize the activities that are most beneficial and enjoyable for you.

My Self-Care Planner

Ideas for Self-Care Activities:	DATE:
	Today's Area of Focus:
	List of Priorities:
Personal Reminder:	○
	○
	○
	○
	○

- ## Mirror of the Self

Self-reflection activities can be an effective tool for boosting morale in several ways. Self-reflection activities can help you become more aware of your thoughts and feelings. This increased self-awareness can lead to a greater sense of clarity and purpose and can help girls to identify areas for personal growth and improvement. Following are some steps for engaging in a self-reflection activity:

✓ Spend some time sitting quietly and concentrating on your breathing. Allow your mind to settle and your thoughts to slow down.

✓ Choose a prompt or question to reflect on. This can be a general question, like "What do I want out of life?" or a more specific question related to a particular area of your life, like "How can I improve my communication with my friends?"

✓ Write down your feelings and thoughts about the prompt in your journal. Be honest and non-judgmental with yourself.

Mirror of the Self Prompts

1. What are the top three goals I have for my life?

1)	2)	3)

2. What activities do I enjoy doing when I'm alone?

3. What achievement of mine do I consider to be the greatest?

4. What lesson in life has impacted me the most?

5. What accomplishment am I most proud of?

6. Which moment in my life would I like to experience again?

7. Who has been a constant support system for me?

8. What are the actions I need to take to achieve my personal success?

- **The Kindness Crusade**

Acts of kindness can improve the mood of the person receiving the kindness, which can lead to positive emotions and feelings of happiness. This can create a ripple effect, spreading positivity throughout the workplace or community and boosting morale for everyone involved.

Following are some steps to perform this activity:

✓ Begin by brainstorming a list of kind acts that you can do for others.

✓ Choose one or more acts from your list to perform each day.

✓ Keep track of your progress in a journal or on a calendar.

✓ Look for opportunities to perform your chosen act of kindness throughout the day.

✓ Be genuine and sincere in your actions and interactions with others.

✓ Reflect on how you feel after performing each act of kindness.

✓ Share your experiences and encourage others to participate in the activity as well.

✓ Consider making random acts of kindness a regular part of your daily routine.

The Kindness Crusade

Once you perform a "Random Act of Kindness" activity, mark it as completed in the corresponding box.

1	2	3	4
Share your food with your friends	Assist your family with a household task	Help someone carry an object	Donate food to someone in need

5	6	7	8
Send a card to someone who is unwell	Write a friendly note to someone	Express your love to someone	Clean an area without being asked

9	10	11	12
Set the table for dinner	Hug a friend	Keep a door open for someone	Reach out to your friends

13	14	15	16
Donate books to a good cause	Give away your pocket money	Participate in baking a cake for neighbours	Offer a compliment to someone

• Spotlight on My Strengths and Weaknesses

An activity focused on strengths, and weaknesses can be important for boosting morale because it helps girls build self-awareness and a more positive self-image. By reflecting on their personal strengths, individuals can build self-confidence and a sense of accomplishment.

Following are some steps for this activity:

✓ Spend some time thinking about your strengths and weaknesses. Think about what comes naturally to you and what you may struggle with.

✓ Write down a list of your strengths and weaknesses. Be honest with yourself and try to list as many as you can.

✓ Review your lists and consider how your strengths and weaknesses have affected your life. Think about how they may have helped or hindered you in achieving your goals.

✓ Identify ways you can build on your strengths and work on your weaknesses. For example, you may want to take a course to improve a specific skill or seek feedback from others to identify areas for improvement.

✓ Create a plan to build on your strengths and work on your weaknesses. Set specific, achievable goals and establish a timeline for achieving them.

Spotlight on My Strengths and Weaknesses

DATE: _____

List of My Top Ten Strengths:

1: _____
2: _____
3: _____
4: _____
5: _____
6: _____
7: _____
8: _____
9: _____
10: _____

List of My Top Ten Weaknesses:

1: _____
2: _____
3: _____
4: _____
5: _____
6: _____
7: _____
8: _____
9: _____
10: _____

A Weakness That I Turned Into a Strength:

_____

_____

One Weakness I Want to Improve and Turn Into a strength:

_____

_____

- **Time Tracking Log**

Time tracker activity can be an effective tool in boosting your morale. It can help you to manage your time efficiently and prioritize your tasks. Here are some steps to follow for time tracker activity:

✓ Start by writing down the time of day that you begin your first activity.

✓ Record the activity that you are doing, as well as any relevant details, such as the location or the people you are with.

✓ Continue to track your activities throughout the day, recording the start and end times of each activity.

✓ Be as detailed as possible in your tracking, and make a note of any interruptions or distractions that occur.

Time Tracking Log

Track the duration of your activities for three consecutive days using this worksheet. Utilize the provided space to record any other activities you engage in.

	DAY 1	DAY 2	DAY 3
Getting ready in the morning			
Breakfast preparation and consumption			
Household chores			
Total duration spent on outdoor activities (e.g., sports, shopping)			
Eating dinner			
Getting ready for bed			

CHAPTER 3 : FROM AWKWARD TO AWESOME: THE ART OF MAKING NEW FRIENDS

Friendship is an essential part of human life, and it is something that can bring great joy and fulfillment. Having strong friendships can help us feel supported and connected and can provide us with a sense of belonging and purpose. However, making and maintaining friendships is not always easy. It takes effort and skill to develop and maintain healthy relationships with others.

The first step in mastering the art of making friends is to understand the importance of friendship. Friendships can have a significant impact on our mental and emotional well-being. Studies have shown that girls with strong social connections are generally happier, healthier, and more resilient than those who lack these connections. Strong friendships can also provide us with a sense of security and stability, as well as a sounding board for our thoughts and ideas.

It is crucial to note that not all friendships are created equal. Some friendships may be more casual or situational, while others may be deeper and more meaningful. Regardless of the type of friendship, it is important to cultivate and maintain these connections over time.

In this chapter, we will explore the different aspects of the art of making friends, from meeting new people to building and sustaining long-lasting friendships. With a little effort and practice, anyone can master the art of making friends and enjoy the benefits that come with strong social connections.

3.1 The Power of Friendships: Why Making Social Connections is so important?

The influence of friendships on your happiness and mental health is significant. Stress is reduced, comfort and delight are given, and loneliness and isolation are avoided by having good companions. Lack of social interaction might be as dangerous as smoking or living a sedentary lifestyle. According to a Swedish study, having a large social network and engaging in physical exercise both help you live longer. As a teen girl, social connections are incredibly important for many reasons. Not only do they provide a sense of belonging and support, but they also help shape your identity and prepare you for adulthood. Here are some creative ways to understand the importance of social connections as a teen girl:

Some of the main explanations for why social ties are so crucial are as follows:

- **Social Connections Provide Emotional Support:**

Being a teenager can be a rollercoaster of emotions, and having a solid social network can help you navigate those ups and downs. Social relationships provide you the comfort and support you need to get through challenging situations, whether it's a friend to vent to or a shoulder to weep on.

- **Building a Support Network:**

One of the key benefits of social connections is building a strong support network of people who care about you and are there for you when you need them. These relationships can be with family members, friends, teachers, mentors, or anyone else who supports your growth and development. A support network can help you navigate the challenges of adolescence and build resilience.

- **Discovering New Perspectives:**

 Social connections can expose you to new perspectives and ideas, which can help you grow as a person. Meeting people from different backgrounds, cultures, and experiences can broaden your horizons and help you build empathy and understanding for others.

- **Creating Lifelong Friendships:**

Social connections can lead to lifelong friendships that can enrich your life for years to come. The friendships you make as a teen can be some of the most meaningful and long-lasting relationships you will ever have.

3.2 The Social Butterfly in Making: Tips and Tricks to make New Friends.

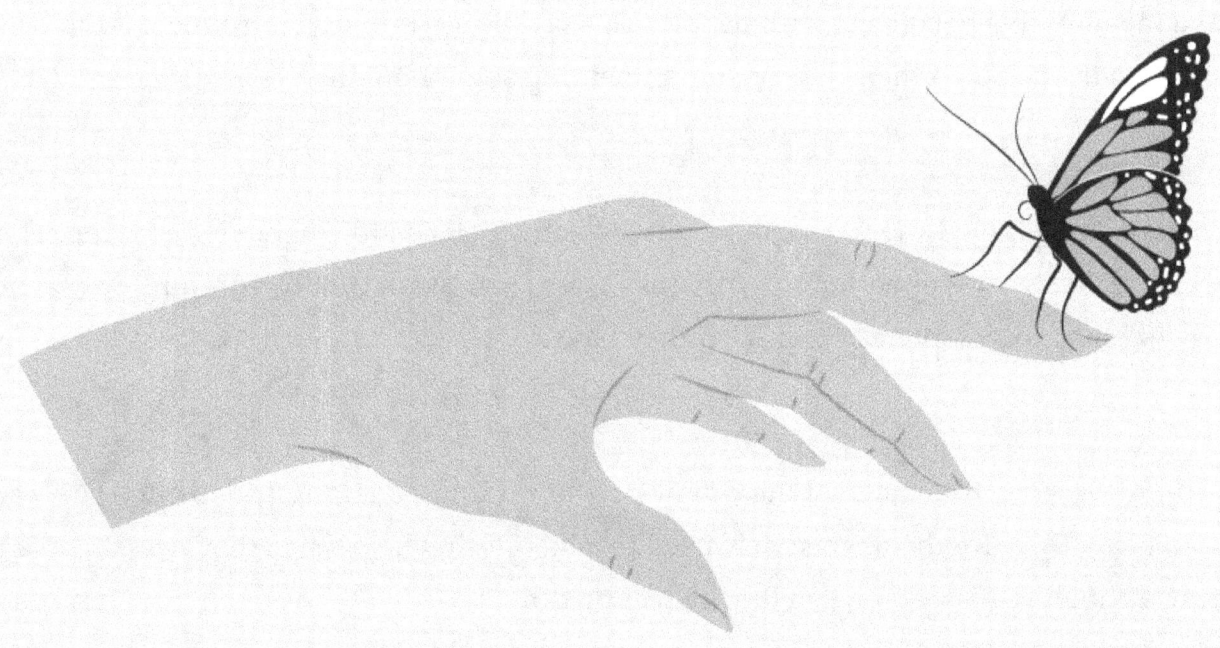

Life without friendship is similar to boring, flavorless, and unpleasant food without spice. You have a sense of belonging when you have friends because you share affection and connection with them. It's crucial to consider maintaining your life's priceless friendships or making new ones.

Following are some tips if you want to make friends:

- **Find Common Interests:**

Look for opportunities to meet new people who share your interests. This can be a great way to connect with others and find people whom you have things in common with. A wonderful method to meet new people who share your interests is through enrolling in a class, going to a social event, or joining a club at school.

- **Be Approachable:**

Make sure you come across as approachable to others. People are more inclined to approach you if you greet them with a smile. It's also important to be respectful and friendly to others, even if they don't seem like they share your interests.

- **Take the Initiative:**

Take the initiative to connect with people. This can be as simple as introducing yourself, asking someone about their day, or complimenting something they're wearing.

- **Listen Actively:**

When you're talking to someone, make sure to actively listen to what they're saying. This means really paying attention to what they're saying, asking follow-up questions, and showing that you're interested in what they have to say.

- **Be Supportive:**

Supporting your friends is an important part of building a strong friendship. This can mean being there for them when they need to talk, offering help when they need it, or just being a shoulder to cry on when they're feeling down.

- **Communicate Effectively:**

The foundation of each connection, including friendships, is effective communication. Make sure to be clear, honest, and respectful when you're communicating with others. Avoid gossiping or talking negatively about others, as this can damage your relationships and make people less likely to trust you.

- **Embrace Differences**

Everyone is unique, and it's important to embrace these differences when building friendships. Instead of focusing on what makes you different from someone else, try to appreciate the things that you have in common and be open to learning from others.

- **Be Kind:**

Being kind to others is a crucial part of building positive relationships. This means being friendly and respectful to everyone, even if you don't necessarily see yourself becoming close friends with them.

- **Have Fun:**

Finally, don't forget to have fun! Friendship is meant to be enjoyable, so make sure to do things that you and your friends enjoy together. This can be anything from going to the movies or a concert to just hanging out and talking.

3.3 Get Social: The Activity Toolkit You Need for Making New Friends

Following are some activities that will help you make new friends:

- **All About Me**

"All About Me" activity can be a simple and effective way to break the ice with new people and start conversations. You may discover common ground and create new connections by learning about people and sharing information about yourself. Following are some steps to perform this activity.

✓ Create a worksheet with questions that help you describe yourself. These questions can include your favorite books, movies, TV shows, music, hobbies, and interests.

✓ Fill out the worksheet with your answers, and make sure, to be honest, and specific about your likes and dislikes.

✓ Share the worksheet with new people you meet as a way to start conversations and get to know each other better.

✓ Encourage the people you meet to fill out a similar worksheet to share with you, so you can get to know them better as well.

✓ Use the information on the worksheet to find common interests and topics to talk about with new people, which can help you develop deeper connections and friendships.

All About Me

Name: _____   My Birthday is _____

I'm really looking forward to this year because

_____

Three words that describe me

_____

_____

_____

In my spare time, I like to ...

_____

_____

_____

_____

_____

_____

_____

My Favourite Things

Color _____

Book _____

Food _____

Subject _____

Hobby _____

Place to visit _____

Sport _____

Store _____

In the future, I would like to ...

_____

_____

_____

_____

_____

_____

_____

- ### Find Someone Who...

"Find Someone Who" is a popular ice-breaking activity that encourages teen girls to interact and connect with one another by finding commonalities and shared experiences.

Following are some steps for this activity:

✓ Write down a list of fun and interesting things you like to do, your hobbies, and your favorite music or TV shows.

✓ Create a sheet with a list of questions based on your interests, such as "Find someone who likes to read mystery novels" or "Find someone who enjoys playing basketball."

✓ Take the sheet and go to places where you can meet new people, such as school events or community centers.

✓ Approach people and ask them the questions on the sheet, and if they answer "yes," mark their name down on the sheet.

✓ If they answer "no," don't worry about it; just move on to the next person.

✓ Once you have completed the sheet, you will have a list of people who share similar interests as you, which will make it easier for you to strike up a conversation and form a new friendship.

Find Someone Who.....

Walk around the classroom, and ask your classmates questions to find someone who fits each statement below.

- You can only find one person for each category.
- You cannot use the same person twice

	NAME
Loves Cooking.	
Enjoys listening to music.	
Adores animals.	
Dislikes exercising.	
Possesses blue eyes.	
Has two sisters.	
Uses an iPhone.	
Loves dancing.	
Regularly drinks coffee.	
Consumes fruit daily.	
Goes to bed very late at night.	
Likes to watch movie in the cinema.	
Prefers eating fish.	
Owns a pet.	

- **Friends Bucket Checklist**

The friends' bucket list is an activity that helps teen girls build and maintain friendships. It involves creating a list of fun activities to do with friends and then setting out to complete them together.

Following are some steps of this activity:

✓ Brainstorm a list of activities or experiences you want to have with your friends.

✓ Choose 10-15 items from your brainstormed list that you would like to achieve with your friends.

✓ Write down these items on a piece of paper as your "Friends Bucket Checklist."

✓ Share your list with your friends and see if they have any additional ideas.

✓ Create a plan with your friends to achieve these items on the checklist, whether it's by scheduling specific dates or making a to-do list.

✓ Work with your friends to check off each item on the checklist as you complete it.

✓ Celebrate your accomplishments with your friends once you have completed all the items on your list.

Friends Bucket Checklist

Develop a strategy with your friends to accomplish the tasks on this checklist and mark off each item as you finish it.

Spend an entire day in each other's company		Volunteer together for a cause you both care about	
Enjoy a relaxing day at the spa		Get a manicure or pedicure together	
Attend a music festival together		Make prank calls to your friends	
Embark on a road trip		Go on a camping trip	
Surprise each other with a party		Read the same book together and discuss it	
Try out a new craft project together		Talk about your future plans and make goals together	
Laugh uncontrollably until you shed tears		Bake something delicious together	
Go on a shopping spree together for a whole day		Do each other's nails as a fun activity	

• Getting to Know You

Getting to know you" activities are important because they allow girls to establish connections and build relationships with one another. This activity provides a comfortable and informal way for people to share information about themselves, their interests, and their backgrounds, which can help break down barriers and build trust.

Following are some steps of this activity:

✓ Create a list of fun and engaging questions that you can ask a new friend or acquaintance to help get to know them better. This could include their favorite hobbies, interests, or books they like to read.

✓ Use these questions to start a conversation and make a connection with the person. Remember to actively listen to their responses and ask follow-up questions to show your interest.

✓ Be open and honest in your own answers to these questions. This will help build trust and encourage the other person to be open with you as well.

✓ Take note of any common interests or experiences you share, as these can be great conversation starters for future interactions.

GETTING TO KNOW YOU

Listed below are some questions that you could ask to get to know a friend better: Write the answers on the line!

What are some of your favourite hobbies or interests?

_____

Do you have any pets or siblings?

_____

Have you traveled anywhere interesting recently?

_____

What is your favourite type of music or artist?

_____

What are your favourite movies or TV shows?

_____

Have you read any good books lately?

_____

What do you like to do in your free time?

_____

Do you play any sports or have a favourite team?

_____

Have you been to any concerts or festivals?

_____

Do you have any favourite foods or restaurants?

_____

- Two Truths and a Lie:

This activity involves each person sharing three statements about themselves, with two being true and one being a lie. The other participants must guess which statement is the lie, and then the person reveals the correct answer. This activity can be a fun and effective way to help individuals get to know each other and build connections.

TWO TRUTHS AND A LIE	
Name: _____	Date: _____
Write down three statements about yourself. Two of those statements should be true and one should be a lie. See if your friends can guess which statement is true.	
1.	
2.	
3.	

- **Interview a Friend**

The activity can help deepen friendships by allowing teen girls to learn more about their friends, their perspectives, and their experiences. This can help build trust and understanding.

Following are some steps of this activity:

✓ Choose a friend whom you would like to interview.

✓ Prepare a list of questions you want to ask your friend.

✓ Find a quiet and comfortable place to conduct the interview.

✓ Start the interview by introducing yourself and explaining the purpose of the activity.

✓ Ask your friend the questions on your list and actively listen to their responses.

✓ Ask follow-up questions to gain a deeper understanding of their answers.

✓ Take notes during the interview to help you remember important details.

✓ Use your notes to reflect on what you learned about your friend and the experience of conducting an interview.

✓ Consider sharing your experience with others, such as in a class discussion or with a family member.

Interview a Friend

Conduct an interview with your friend and inquire about their areas of interest, family, academic pursuits, hobbies, and aspirations for the future. Don't hesitate to ask additional questions to delve deeper into their responses.

Date: _____

Question: _____

_____

Answer: _____

_____

_____

Question: _____

_____

Answer: _____

_____

_____

Question: _____

_____

Answer: _____

_____

_____

Question: _____

_____

Answer: _____

_____

_____

- ## Conversation Starters

The activity can promote communication between individuals who may not know each other well or are uncomfortable initiating conversations. The use of conversation starters can help break the ice and create an environment where people feel comfortable sharing their thoughts and ideas.

Following are some steps of this activity:

✓ Prepare a list of conversation starters that are appropriate for your group and setting. These can be simple questions or statements that encourage participants to share their thoughts and feelings.

✓ Gather the group together and explain the activity. Let them know that you will be sharing the conversation starters and that they can take turns answering or responding to them.

✓ Pass out the list of conversation starters to each participant, or project them on a screen for the group to see.

- ## Compliment Cards

Each participant should write their name on a sheet of paper and distribute it to the other participants. Each person will then write a compliment or positive message about the person whose name is on the paper. This is a great way to build self-esteem and positive relationships.

CHAPTER 4 : GETTING OUT OF YOUR SHELL : TAKING YOUR SOCIAL LIFE TO THE NEXT LEVEL

As a teen girl, you are going through a period of significant change in your life. You are transitioning from childhood to adulthood and navigating complex social, emotional, and cognitive challenges. Social life plays an essential role in helping you develop the skills and knowledge necessary to navigate this period successfully. Social life refers to the interactions and relationships that you have with other people. It encompasses a wide range of activities, such as spending time with friends, participating in extracurricular activities, and engaging in community service. These activities provide you with opportunities to develop your social, emotional, and cognitive abilities.

The importance of social life cannot be overstated. Social connections provide us with a sense of belonging and can help to reduce feelings of loneliness and isolation. Being part of a community and having a support network can also help to improve our mental health and provide us with a greater sense of purpose. Studies have shown that girls who have strong social networks are generally happier and healthier than those who do not. For instance, research has shown that teen girls who have regular social interactions tend to have better cognitive functions and are less likely to develop dementia in later life. Social connections can also help to reduce stress and improve our overall quality of life. In this chapter, we will explore some tips and activities that will help you take your social life to the next level.

4.1 What's Holding You Back? Identifying Potential Barriers in Socializing.

Barriers in socializing can refer to factors that make it challenging or difficult for people to form social connections and interact with others. Here are some common barriers to socializing:

- **Social Anxiety:**

Social anxiety can make it challenging for girls to feel comfortable in social situations, leading them to avoid socializing or to feel very anxious and uncomfortable when socializing.

- **Language Barriers:**

Girls who do not speak the same language may struggle to communicate and connect with one another, creating a barrier to socializing.

- **Cultural Differences:**

Cultural differences can make it challenging for girls to understand one another and form meaningful connections. Differences in social norms, values, and traditions can lead to misunderstandings and barriers to socializing.

- **Lack of Social Skills:**

Some girls may not have developed social skills, such as initiating and maintaining conversations, reading social cues, and expressing themselves effectively. This can make it challenging for them to connect with others and form social relationships.

- ## Physical Limitations:

Physical disabilities or limitations can make it difficult for some girls to access certain social spaces or activities, creating a barrier to socializing.

- ## Mental Health Issues:

Mental health issues, such as depression or anxiety, can make it challenging for teen girls to socialize and connect with others.

- ## Discrimination and Prejudice:

Discrimination and prejudice can create barriers for girls to socialize and form relationships with others who belong to different ethnic, cultural, or social groups

- ## Lack Of Confidence:

Teen girls who lack confidence in their social skills or ability to connect with others may avoid social situations or struggle to initiate conversations and form relationships.

- ## Shyness:

Shyness can make it difficult for teen girls to put themselves out there and initiate conversations or social interactions.

4.2 Building Bridges, Not Walls: Tips for Improving Your Social Life

Improving your social life can bring many benefits, including increased happiness, better mental health, and more meaningful connections with others. Here are some tips for improving your social life:

- ## Identify Your Interests:

By identifying your interests, you can find groups or events that revolve around those interests. This can make it easier to find people who share similar hobbies or passions and can lead to more meaningful connections. Some examples of interest-based groups could include a hiking club, a book club, or a cooking class.

- **Attend a Conference or Workshop:**

Conferences and workshops are great opportunities to learn new things, meet new people, and network. Look for events that focus on something you're interested in, such as science, technology, or business.

- **Start a Book Club:**

If you love reading, start a book club with your friends or classmates. You can choose books to read together and then meet up to discuss them. Not only will you make new friends, but you'll also get to share your love of reading with others.

- **Join a Language Exchange Program:**

If you're interested in learning a new language, join a language exchange program. You'll get to practice speaking with native speakers and make new friends from different cultures.

- **Try a New Hobby:**

Trying a new hobby, such as knitting, rock climbing, or playing an instrument, can be a great way to meet new people who share your interests. Look for local classes or groups to join.

- **Host a Potluck:**

Hosting a potluck is a fun and low-key way to get together with friends and classmates. Everyone can bring a dish to share, and you can enjoy a meal together while socializing

- **Attend a Cultural Festival:**

Attending a cultural festival, such as a food festival or music festival, can be a great way to learn about different cultures and make new friends. Look for events in your community and bring some friends along.

- **Participate in a Community Service Project:**

Participating in a community service project, such as cleaning up a park or helping at a food bank, can be a great way to meet new people while making a positive impact in your community.

4.3 Ready, Set, Socialize - A Toolbox of Activities to Improve Your Social Life.

Following are some tools to improve your social life:Social Role-Playing Scenarios

✓ Role play is an important tool to improve social skills because it allows teen girls to practice and experience real-life situations in a safe and controlled environment.

✓ Following are some steps of this activity:

✓ Decide on a topic that you and your friends are interested in exploring. It could be anything from peer pressure or conflict with a friend.

✓ Assign different roles to each participant based on the scenario you have chosen. For example, if you have chosen to explore the topic of peer pressure, you can assign one person to be the peer who is pressuring another person and the other person to be the one who is feeling pressured.

✓ Establish the setting and the circumstances surrounding the scenario. This will help you and your friends to understand the context of the situation and act accordingly.

✓ Once the scene is set, each person should begin to act out their role in the scenario. Try to stay in character and respond to each other as you think your character would in real life.

✓ If you have time, you can also switch roles and try the scenario again from a different perspective. This can help you to gain a better understanding of the situation and develop empathy for others.

Social Role Playing Scenarios

Imagine you and your friend want to explore setting healthy boundaries in your friendship, such as respecting each other's privacy or time. Your role is to communicate your needs, listen to your friend's perspective, and work towards a mutually respectful agreement. How do you navigate the conversation in a way that is respectful and effective?

Imagine you and your friend want to explore ways to speak out against injustice or discrimination, such as racism or sexism. Your role is to brainstorm effective ways to make a positive impact, such as organising a protest or volunteering for a community organisation. How do you work together to create change?

Imagine you and your friend want to explore different cultures and learn more about the world around you. Your role is to plan cultural activities, such as trying new foods or attending cultural events, and to learn from each other's experiences and perspectives. How do you approach cultural differences in a way that is respectful and open-minded?

Imagine you and your friend want to explore ways to build self-esteem and self-confidence. Your role is to support each other in setting goals, celebrating accomplishments, and practicing self-care. How do you encourage each other to grow and thrive as individuals?

Imagine you and your friend want to explore ways to manage stress and improve mental health. Your role is to share coping strategies, such as mindfulness or exercise, and to provide emotional support during difficult times. How do you prioritise your mental health and support each other's well-being?

- Empathy Map

The empathy map activity can be an effective tool for improving social life because it helps teen girls develop their empathy skills and better understand the perspective of others.

Following are some steps of this activity:

✓ Choose the individual or group for which you wish to grow your empathy. It may be a close friend, a member of your family, or a bunch of strangers.

✓ In the "Says" section of the empathy map, write down what the person or group has said, such as their thoughts or opinions. This could include things that you have heard them say directly or things that you have observed about them.

✓ In the "Thinks" section of the empathy map, write down what the person or group might be thinking, such as their beliefs or assumptions. This could include things that you have heard them express or things that you have inferred from their actions.

✓ In the "Feels" section of the empathy map, write down what the person or group might be feeling, such as their emotions or moods. This could include things that you have observed about their body language or things that they have expressed directly.

✓ In the "Does" section of the empathy map, write down what the person or group does, such as their actions or behaviors. This could include things that you have observed about their behavior or things that they have told you about their actions.

✓ Reflect on the person or group. Reflect on the information that you have written down in the empathy map. What insights or observations have you gained about the person or group? What new perspectives have you developed?

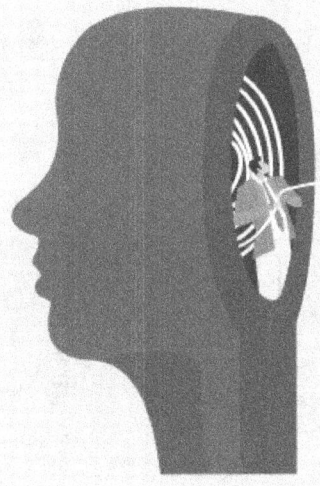
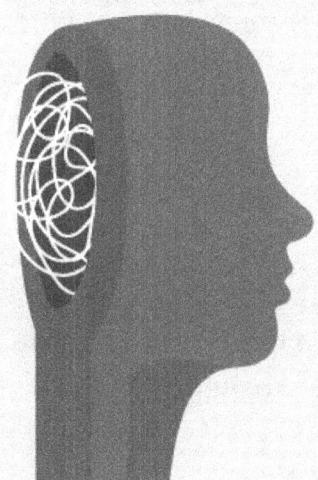

Empty Map

Says

What do you hear them saying?

What do they talk about?

Thinks

What are they worried/excited about?

What are they thinking about?

Who

Name

Does

What are their daily activities
(at home or at school school)?

Feels

How do they feel on a daily basis?

Pain

What are their frustrations and
challenges?

Gain

What are their goals?

What makes them happy?

- **Social Anxiety Challenge Prompt**

This activity includes prompts that challenge girls to face their social anxiety and push themselves out of their comfort zone.

Following are some steps of this activity:

✓ Think about the specific social situation or fear that triggers your anxiety. For example, it could be public speaking, meeting new people, or attending social events.

✓ Select a challenge prompt that will help you confront and overcome your social anxiety. The prompt should be specific, measurable, and achievable. For example, "I will attend a networking event and talk to at least three new people" or "I will give a presentation to a small group of colleagues."

✓ Plan the steps you will take to achieve the challenge prompt. This might include practicing your presentation, researching conversation starters, or rehearsing positive self-talk.

✓ Imagine yourself successfully completing the challenge and visualize how it would feel. This can help you build confidence and motivation to overcome your social anxiety.

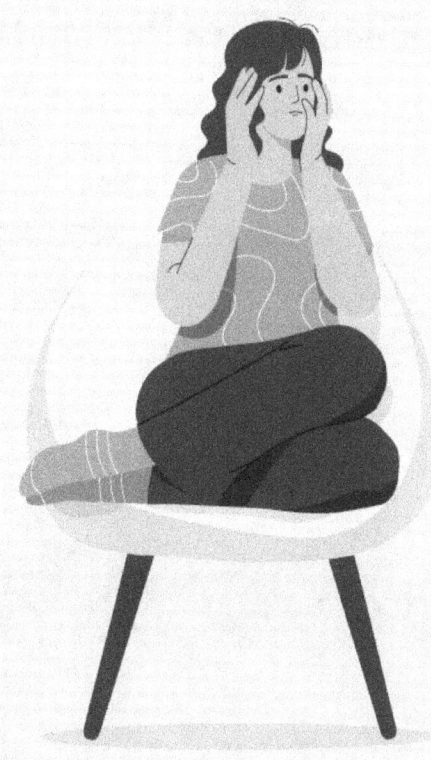

Social Anxiety Challenge Prompt

Begin with the least frightening task and gradually progress to more challenging ones.

1. Go for a walk alone.

2. Dress in something outside your usual style.

3. Reconnect with an old friend.

4. Sustain eye contact while conversing.

5. Sit in a crowded waiting room

6. Order a menu item without preplanning your selection.

7. Strike up a conversation with a new neighbour you encounter on the sidewalk.

8. Walk in a busy mall

9. Attend a family gathering.

10. Host a dinner party for friends.

11. Pose a question during a class discussion.

12. Do public speaking

- **Mind Mapping**

You may use this activity to build a visual representation of your social life that will help you spot opportunities to practice your social skills, meet new people, and try out new things.Following are some steps of this activity:

✓ Begin by creating a central idea or theme for your mind map, such as "my social life."

✓ Next, brainstorm all the different aspects of your social life that you can think of, such as your hobbies, interests, goals, and current social network.

✓ Once you have a list of different aspects, organize them into different categories or clusters. For example, you might have a cluster for hobbies, a cluster for goals, and a cluster for friends and acquaintances.

✓ Use lines or arrows to connect related items and show how they are linked to each other. For example, you might connect your love of hiking to a group of friends who also enjoy hiking.

✓ Review your mind map and identify areas where you can expand your social circle or try new activities.

- **Volunteer Work:**

This activity involves volunteering your time and skills to a cause or organization that you care about. This can help you meet new people, expand your social circle, and give back to your community.

- ## My Core Values

The essential ideas and beliefs that direct your behavior and activities are known as core values. Knowing what your core values are can help you navigate social settings and make decisions that are consistent with who you really are.

Following are some steps of this activity:

✓ Start by reflecting on your personal values and beliefs. This can include things like honesty, respect, kindness, and empathy.

✓ Write down a list of your core values on a piece of paper or in a notebook.

✓ Review your list of core values and identify the ones that are essential to you.

✓ Think about how your core values can guide your behavior in social situations. For example, if honesty is one of your core values, think about how you can be more truthful and authentic in your interactions with others.

- ## Mindful Breathing:

This activity involves practicing deep, slow breathing to help you stay calm and focused during social interactions. This can help you improve your communication and build stronger connections with others.

Following are some steps of this activity:

✓ Start by finding a quiet space where you can focus and relax without any distractions.

✓ Breathe in slowly and deeply, using your nose to inhale and your mouth to exhale. Always inhale through your diaphragm rather than your chest.

✓ Focus your attention on your breath. Feel the air flowing in and out of your nose, and pay close attention to the sensations in your body as you exhale and inhale.

✓ Count each breath as you exhale, starting with one and counting up to ten. If you lose track, start over at one.

✓ Practice this mindful breathing exercise for a few minutes each day to help improve your ability to stay calm and focused during social interactions.

- **My Social Support Network**

This activity can help you understand the importance of having a strong social support network and how it can be helpful in improving social skills. By building strong connections with others, teen girls can feel more confident in social situations and better able to handle social challenges.

Following are some steps of this activity:

✓ Start by identifying the people in your life who provide you with emotional support. This may include family members or friends.

✓ Make a list of your needs, such as emotional support, practical advice, or someone to listen to. This will help you communicate your needs more effectively to your support network.

✓ Practice communicating your needs to your support network. Let them know how they can help and what you need from them.

- **Social Decision-Making:**

Create a scenario where the group has to make a social decision, such as where to go for a group outing or how to resolve a conflict. Have each person share their opinion and work together to come to a decision. This activity helps build communication, collaboration, and decision-making skills.

- **Compliment Circle**

This activity helps build positivity, empathy, and relationship-building skills. Following are some steps of this activity:

✓ Sit in a circle with your group, facing each other.

✓ Explain to the group that you will be doing a compliment circle, where each person will give a genuine compliment to the person to their right.

✓ Emphasize that the compliments should be specific, genuine, and uplifting. Encourage the group to think about the person's positive qualities and express their appreciation.

✓ Begin the compliment circle by having one person start by giving a compliment to the person on their right.

✓ After the first person gives their compliment, the next person in the circle gives a compliment to the person on their right, and so on.

✓ Continue the circle until each person has received a compliment from the person on their right.

✓ After everyone has had a chance to give and receive compliments, take a moment to discuss the activity as a group. Ask participants to share how they felt about giving and receiving compliments and how they can incorporate more positivity and appreciation in their daily lives.

CHAPTER 5 : THE CONFIDENCE CODE : UNLOCKING YOUR POTENTIAL WITH SELF CONFIDENCE AND SELF ESTEEM

"One may create a better world with self-awareness and confidence in one's own abilities."

Self-confidence and self-esteem are two related but distinct concepts that are important for teen girls. Self-confidence refers to a belief in oneself and one's abilities, while self-esteem refers to one's overall sense of self-worth and value. Self-confidence involves feeling sure of yourself in social situations, speaking up for yourself and expressing your opinions, and feeling capable of handling challenges and setbacks. On the other hand, self-esteem involves feeling good about yourself, valuing your unique qualities and strengths, and having a positive overall view of yourself.

A variety of factors, including your upbringing, your experiences in school and with friends, and your own internal thought patterns and self-talk, can influence both self-confidence and self-esteem. Developing healthy self-confidence and self-esteem is essential for your overall well-being and can help you feel more upbeat and resilient in the face of challenges.

People frequently believe that confidence is something that you either have or don't have, but it is a quality you acquire through knowledge and experience; it is not one you are born with. When your accomplishments outweigh your negative self-perception, you develop confidence. That comes naturally to certain people. Others, though, find it difficult to comprehend how to boost their confidence. Yet when we have strong self-confidence, we can live our lives without being concerned about failure or setbacks. Confident individuals are completely aware of their skills and the importance of their accomplishments, but they also realize that they don't know everything and can't do everything perfectly. While it can be difficult to describe, self-confidence often refers to a feeling of comfort with oneself and one's instincts, as well as the conviction that one can rely on one's own skills, knowledge, and judgment. Teen girls who are confident, accept new challenges since they are confident in their ability to meet them. They'll give it their all and are driven to achieve their objectives without giving them too much thought or internal reflection. They handle life's challenges with confidence and calm. Those who are confident congratulate others and feel real delight for them rather than feeling jealous or resentful towards their accomplishment. They are motivated to pick up all knowledge they can about other people's success. They don't explain away their own shortcomings or the accomplishments of others. They maintain a growth attitude even though they are not always optimistic. They frequently recognize the humor in their mistakes, making them more inclined to chuckle in response and quickly get over embarrassment or guilt

Journey of some Teen Girls towards Confidence

• Sarah's Story:

Sarah was always conscious of her weight and how she looked in clothes. Her peers often teased her for being too thin or too curvy, depending on the day. She felt like she couldn't win and would often wear baggy clothes to try and hide her body. One day, she decided to try on a dress that she had been eyeing for weeks but was too scared to wear. To her surprise, she loved how it looked on her and felt confident in her skin for the first time in many years. She realized it didn't matter what others thought of her body as long as she felt comfortable and confident in her skin.

• Lily's Story:

Lily struggled with acne throughout her teenage years, which made her feel self-conscious about her appearance. She would often wear a lot of makeup to try and cover up her blemishes, but this only made her feel worse. One day, she decided to go out without any makeup on and realized that people didn't treat her any differently. She realized that her acne didn't define her and that she was more than her appearance. She began to focus on taking care of her skin rather than covering it up and felt more confident in her natural beauty.

• Maya's Story:

Maya had always been tall and skinny, which made her feel self-conscious about her body. She would often wear clothes that were too big for her to try and hide her thin frame. However, one day, she tried on a crop top and realized that she loved the way it looked on her. She realized that being thin wasn't bad and that she could still look great in clothes that fit her properly. She began to embrace her body and started wearing clothes that made her feel confident, regardless of what others thought.

These stories show that confidence comes from within and that embracing your unique beauty is essential. Whether wearing clothes that make you feel comfortable or taking care of your skin, it's essential to focus on what makes you feel confident in your skin.

5.1 The Hidden Culprits: Uncovering the Causes of Low Self-Confidence and Self-Esteem.

As a teen, you may face many challenges that can impact your self-confidence and self-esteem. It's important to recognize these barriers and work to overcome them so that you can feel positive and self-assured in all aspects of your life.

Following are some causes of low self-confidence and self-esteem

- ## Negative Self-Talk:

Negative self-talk can be a real challenge for many teens. It's that little voice inside your head that tells you that you're not good enough, that you're not smart enough, or that you're not worthy. This kind of self-talk can be incredibly damaging to your self-esteem and can make it hard to build self-confidence. It's important to recognize when you're engaging in negative self-talk and to challenge those thoughts with positive affirmations.

- ## Comparison to Others:

In today's world, it's easy to fall into the trap of comparing yourself to others. Social media can be a particularly challenging environment when it comes to comparisons. It's important to remember that people tend to share only their best moments on social media and that what you see on your feed is not an accurate representation of reality. Instead of focusing on what others are doing, focus on your own progress and accomplishments.

- ## Social Media:

Social media may be a fantastic tool for maintaining friendships and expressing yourself, but it can also be a source of anxiety and unhappiness. It's critical to be aware of how much time you spend on social media and to take precautions to reduce your exposure to potentially hazardous interactions or information.

- ## Bullying:

Bullying can take many forms, from name-calling and teasing to more serious forms of harassment. If you are experiencing bullying, it can be incredibly damaging to your self-esteem and can make it challenging to build self-confidence. It's essential to seek help from a trusted adult or mental health professional if you are being bullied.

- ## Family Dynamics:

Family dynamics can play a significant role in developing self-confidence and self-esteem. If you have parents or other family members who are overly critical or who don't provide enough support, it can be a barrier to building self-confidence. It's essential to seek out positive influences in your life, such as mentors, friends, or teachers, who can provide support and guidance.

5.2 No More Negative Self Talk: Overcoming the Barriers of Self-Confidence and Self-Esteem.

Here are some tips for overcoming the barriers to self-confidence and self-esteem.

- **Focus on Your Strengths:**

 Everyone has unique talents and abilities. So, rather than comparing yourself to others, concentrate on your own strengths and what makes you unique.

- **Embrace Failure as a Learning Opportunity:**

Everyone fails at some point. Instead of dwelling on your failures, see them as opportunities to learn and grow.

- **Practice Self-Care:**

By consuming a well-balanced diet, engaging in regular exercise, and getting adequate sleep, you may take good care of your mental and physical health. Spend time engaging in activities that make you feel good, such as hobbies or socializing with friends.

- **Set Achievable Goals:**

Identify something you want to achieve, and then break it down into smaller, achievable steps. Celebrate your achievements along the way, and don't be too hard on yourself if you experience setbacks.

- **Challenge Negative Self-Talk:**

As you see negative thoughts starting to creep in, combat them by determining if they are actually true. If not, replace them with positive affirmations.

- **Surround Yourself With Positive Influences:**

Spend time with people who encourage and support you, and distance yourself from those who bring you down or make you feel bad about yourself.

- **Take Risks:**

Step outside of your comfort bubble and try new things, even if they scare you. The more you push yourself to try new things, the more confident you will become.

- **Practice Self-Compassion:**

Be kind to yourself, and treat yourself the way you would treat a good friend. Remember that everyone makes mistakes and that it's okay to fail sometimes

5.3 The Empowered You: An Activity Toolkit to Boost your Self-Confidence and Self Esteem

Following are some activities to boost your self-confidence and self-esteem:

- **Certificate of Accomplishment**

✓ List some things you would like to achieve or improve in your life, such as academic or personal goals.

✓ Choose one of these goals and create an action plan with specific steps that you can take to achieve it.

✓ Take action and start working towards your goal.

✓ When you have made significant progress or achieved your goal, write a reflection on what you have accomplished and how it has impacted your life.

✓ Design a certificate of accomplishment, either by hand or using a computer, to recognize and celebrate your achievement.

✓ Share your accomplishment with others, such as friends or family members, to receive encouragement and support.

CERTIFICATE
OF
ACCOMPLISHMENT

This certificate of accomplishment is hereby granted to:

_____

_____

For the accomplishment of:

_____

_____

Keep up the
great work

_____
By

_____
Date

- ## Self Esteem Journal

✓ Get a journal or notebook that you will use to record your thoughts and feelings.

✓ Set aside sometime each day to work on your journal. This can be in the morning or before bed, whatever works best for you.

✓ Think about a positive experience you had that day or something you accomplished that you are proud of.

✓ Write down your thoughts and feelings about that experience. Be specific and describe how it made you feel.

✓ Reflect on any negative thoughts or feelings you may have had throughout the day and write them down. Challenge any negative self-talk with positive self-talk. At the end of each week, review your journal and reflect on your progress. Celebrate your accomplishments and think about what you can do to continue building your self-esteem.

Daily Self- Esteem Journal
Use this form to check in with yourself about your current emotions and well-being.
1. Today, something good that happened to me was...
2. Something positive someone said to me today was:
3. A compliment that someone gave me today was:
4. A compliment that I would like to give myself today is:
5. Positive emotions that I felt today were:
6. I brought joy to someone else when:
7. I had a negative thought about myself when:

- ## You-nique!

This activity helps you recognize and appreciate your individual qualities and helps boost your confidence by emphasizing your strengths.

✓ Think about what makes you unique and special as a person. This can be a talent, a personality trait, a physical characteristic, or something else entirely.

✓ Write down your unique qualities on a piece of paper or index card.

✓ Decorate your paper or index card with drawings, stickers, or other designs that represent your unique qualities.

✓ Share your "You-nique" qualities with the group or a trusted friend.

✓ Keep your "You-nique" card or paper in a special place where you can see it every day as a reminder of your strengths and unique qualities.

You-nique!

Embrace your individuality! Being unique implies that you possess distinct qualities that set you apart from others. Can you identify ten positive attributes that make you exceptional? This could encompass your talents, traits, or experiences that make you stand out.

1: _____

2: _____

3: _____

4: _____

5: _____

6: _____

7: _____

• Reframing Negative Talk

Reframing negative self-talk is an effective activity to boost confidence because our thoughts have a significant impact on our emotions and behaviors. When we consistently engage in negative self-talk, it can lower our self-esteem and make us more hesitant to try new things or take on new challenges. By reframing negative self-talk into positive or neutral statements, we can change the way we think about ourselves and our abilities. Following are some steps of this activity:

✓ Identify negative self-talk patterns: Write down any negative thoughts that come to mind.

✓ Evaluate the truth of the negative thought: Ask yourself if the negative thought is really true or if it's just a perception.

✓ Reframe the negative thought: Turn the negative thought into a positive one. For example, if the negative thought is "I'm not good enough," reframe it to "I have strengths and skills that make me unique and valuable."

Reframing Negative Self-Talk	
Name: _____	Date: _____
Negative Self-Talk Statement	Reframing Positive Self-Talk Statement

• Self-Esteem Sentence Completion

Self-esteem sentence completion activity is an effective tool to help people girls self-awareness and improve their self-esteem. By completing sentences that start with positive affirmations, girls are encouraged to think positively and reflect on their self-worth.

Following are the steps of this activity:

✓ Start by writing down the beginning of a sentence that relates to your self-esteem, such as "I feel good about myself when…"

✓ Complete the sentence with as many positive endings as possible, such as "I accomplish something I've been working on" or "I express myself creatively."

✓ Take some time to reflect on the positive traits and actions that you've written down and recognize the strengths and achievements that make you unique.

✓ If you find it difficult to come up with positive endings to the sentence, think about the support you receive from family and friends or consider seeking help from a counselor or therapist to address any underlying issues.

Self-Esteem Sentences Completion

I enjoy assisting with...

My greatest talent is...

I feel a sense of pride when..

My favourite skill is...

People appreciate it when I...

I experience the most joy when...

I enjoy aiding others with...

I feel confident when I...

- **Letter to Future Self**

This activity is essential for boosting confidence as it helps you to envision a positive future for yourself and identify the steps you need to take to get there. Writing down your aspirations and reading them back to yourself can also serve as a powerful reminder of your own potential and ability to achieve your goals.

✓ Set aside some time to reflect about your future goals and ideal self.

✓ Write a letter to your future self, describing how you want to feel about yourself and what you hope to achieve.

✓ Be specific about the positive changes you want to make in your life and how you will accomplish them.

✓ Use positive affirmations and encouraging words to remind yourself of your strengths and capabilities.

✓ Seal the letter in an envelope and save it in a safe place.

Letter to My Future Self

Use this page to compose a letter to your future self, detailing how you aspire to feel about yourself and the accomplishments you hope to achieve.

Dear _____ .

_____

_____

_____

_____

_____

_____

Sincerely,

- ## I am Someone Who...

This activity helps individuals recognize and celebrate their personal strengths and qualities. By identifying positive characteristics and values that they possess, individuals can build a stronger sense of self-confidence and self-worth.

Following are some steps of this activity:

✓ Begin by identifying your core values, beliefs, and personality traits.

✓ Write down a list of positive statements that start with "I am someone who."

✓ Read the list aloud and internalize the positive affirmations.

✓ Use these statements to guide your actions and behaviors.

✓ Use these statements to counteract negative self-talk.

✓ Visualize yourself embodying these qualities and traits.

✓ Continuously add to the list as you discover new positive traits and qualities about yourself.

✓ Surround yourself with supportive people who also see these positive qualities in you.

I am Someone Who...

This activity is designed to assist teen girls in identifying and celebrating their personal strengths and qualities. Complete the following sentences to share more about yourself:

I am someone who loves _____

I am someone who hates _____

I am someone who can't _____

I am someone who can _____

I am someone who will never _____

I am someone who has _____

I am someone who can't wait to _____

I am someone who has never _____

I am someone who wishes _____

I am someone who tried to _____

I am someone whom everybody seems to _____

I am someone who just can't get enough _____

I am someone who usually forgets to _____

I am someone who never forgets to _____

I am someone who is thankful for _____

WRAPPING UP YOUR JOURNEY.

To all teenage girls out there, navigating the social world can be tough, but it doesn't have to be. The Social Skills for Teen Girls 13-19 survival guide provides a roadmap for building confidence, making friends, and improving self-esteem. It's normal to feel uncertain and anxious about social situations, but remember that you are not alone. Many other girls of your age are going through the same experiences and feelings.

This survival guide starts by helping you identify your strengths and qualities. It also provides tips for challenging negative self-talk and replacing it with positive affirmations.

Recognizing and celebrating your unique traits can give you a sense of self-confidence and help you feel more comfortable in social situations.

Making friends is an essential part of the social world, and this guide has several strategies for building friendships. It encourages you to step out of your comfort zone, participate in activities, and reach out to others. It's important to remember that building friendships takes time and effort, but it's worth it.

Improving self-confidence and self-esteem can be a challenge, but the guide provides practical tips for doing so. It encourages you to practice self-care, surround yourself with positive and supportive people, and reflect on your successes and accomplishments. These strategies can help you build a positive self-image and feel better about yourself.

Finally, the guide emphasizes that social skills are a continuous process. It's important to continue practicing and building these skills throughout your life. Remember to be patient and kind to yourself, and don't be reluctant to ask for help when you need it.

In conclusion, **the book Social Skills for Teen Girls 13-19** survival guide is a valuable resource for building confidence, making friends, and improving self-esteem. With determination and practice, you can develop the skills you need to navigate the social world with ease. You are capable of great things, and we believe in you!